Costa Rica

JADINE

Costa Rica

JADINE

EDITORIAL MANAGEMENT
Raquel López Varela

EDITORIAL COORDINATION
Antonio Manilla

EDITORIAL COORDINATION IN COSTA RICA
Asdrúbal Leiva C.

CONTRIBUTORS
Hans Venier

DOCUMENTATION
Melania Coto O.

PHOTOGRAPHS
David Castañer Gago; cover photograph by Federico Chavarría and photograph on page 103 by Asdrúbal Leiva C.

TEXTS
Asdrúbal Leiva C.

COVER DESING
Fernando Ampudia

DESING AND LAYOUT
Fernando Ampudia y Jorge Garrán

Ediciones Jadine, S. A.

www.edicionesjadine.com
E-mail: info@edicionesjadine.com
P. O. Box: 13894-1000
San José, COSTA RICA
CENTROAMÉRICA

Ctra león-la coruña, km 5 - león

ISBN: 978-9968-9621-9-3
LEGAL DEPOSIT: LE-1472-2007

Printed in Spain - Impreso en España
EDITORIAL EVERGRÁFICAS, S. L.
Ctra. León-La Coruña, km 5
LEÓN (SPAIN)

www.everest.es
Customer information service: +34 902 123 400

Acknowledgements

The elaboration of this book would not have possible without the help of the following institutions and businesses:

• **MUSEO DEL ORO (GOLDEN MUSEUM)** SAN JOSÉ • **MUSEO DEL JADE (JADE MUSEUM)** SAN JOSÉ • **MUSEO NACIONAL (NATIONAL MUSEUM)** SAN JOSÉ • **TEATRO NACIONAL (NATIONAL THEATRE)** SAN JOSÉ • **EAGLE TOURS** LA FORTUNA DE SAN CARLOS • **AVENTURAS ARENAL** LA FORTUNA DE SAN CARLOS • **ECO CENTRO DANAUS** LA FORTUNA DE SAN CARLOS • **SKY ADVENTURE** LA FORTUNA DE SAN CARLOS • **MAWAMBA LODGE** TORTUGUERO • **WATERFALL GARDENS** HEREDIA • **FABRICA DE CARRETAS CHAVERRI (OXCART FACTORY)** SARCHÍ DE VALVERDE VEGA • **RÍOS TROPICALES** SAN JOSÉ • **SKY TREK** MONTEVERDE • **JARDÍN ECOLÓGICO DE EL CASTILLO** LA FORTUNA DE SAN CARLOS • **OCARINA EXPEDICIONES** SAN JOSÉ

Index

Introduction

All of us Costa Ricans feel extremely proud of this small country which, in spite of its multiple problems –those of a country still underdeveloped - has kept up the struggle to become one of the most important tourist destinations at world level, mainly for adventure and nature-related tourism. And that has come to be so because Costa Ricans have traditionally been very friendly and open to those people who visit the country. We just love having people visiting, people who come from all over the world to see the beauty of this land, our customs and our people but mainly, our nature.

This book is meant to show –as any car ride would, our Costa Rica with all its different features, the country such as it is, all across the land, giving priority to the country's treasures, its nature and the wonderful people.

In spite of the fact that the country is politically divided into seven provinces: San José, Alajuela, Cartago, Heredia, Puntarenas and Limón; for practical locating effects, we will divide this book into several regions. These great areas or regions are not formally or officially devised, but they permit the division of the country into more comfortable segments to go over and display for the reader. These regions are: the Central Plateau (which includes the cities of San José, Heredia, Guanacaste, Cartago and Alajuela, as well as their surroundings), the Northwest and Peninsula of Nicoya, (which includes the mountains of the Guanacaste Volcanic Mountain Range, all the way to the Northwest Pacific Ocean coast and the peninsula of Nicoya), the Central Pacific (which includes the area from the city of Puntarenas to the Ballena ("Whale") Marine National Park, towards the southern end of the country, the Northern Plains (which includes the areas contained between the eastern and northern baselines of the Guanacaste Volcanic Mountain Range and Central Mountain Range, respectively), the Caribbean (the Caribbean Basin Coastal Plains, from the San Juan River in the north, all the way down to Panama's northern borderline. And finally, there is the South (which includes all of the country's south-eastern end, from the Talamanca mountain range to the Peninsula of Osa).

Each one of these regions will take up a chapter in this book, with each chapter emphasising and showing the most important and picturesque places, the people and attractions in each of them.

In addition to the regions, we will take a look at important aspects of the land, such as location, climate and geography, its politics and economy, its history, the people, their culture, and the nature.

Impressive view of the mountains at dawn, in the Talamanca range.

Location, climate and geography

Costa Rica, with a territory of only 51,100 Km², only bigger than Belize and El Salvador in Central America, is a tiny country located in the very 'waistline' of the American continent. The lands that it occupies today were a kind of archipelago during the Tertiary age, where the Pacific Ocean and the Caribbean Sea formerly came upon each other. Nevertheless, the intense tectonic and volcanic activity during that period started outlining its volcanic mountain ranges, which presently zigzag the country from side to side.

Typical forest in Rincón of the Vieja. National Park.

Tourist hurling himself through the canopy, amongst the trees, in the vicinity of Arenal volcano.

Papilionidae butterfly. This is only one of the 560 species that inhabit the country.

The fact that it is such a small, narrow land, that it has really high mountain ranges and that it is being continuously showered by the moisture which precipitates with the Caribbean Sea's North Winds, allows it to enjoy a great variety of micro-climates that make it so auspicious a place for hosting a great diversity of fauna and flora.

Bromeliad of bright colours.

Inmense crater of Poás volcano, one of the largest in the world.

NATIONAL PARKS AND REGIONS IN COSTA RICA

1. Arenal
2. Ballena
3. Barra del Colorado y Tortuguero
4. Barra Honda
5. Braulio Carrillo
6. Cabo Blanco
7. Cahuita
8. Caño Negro
9. Carara
10. Corcovado
11. Curú
12. Gandoca-Manzanillo
13. Golfito
14. Guayabo
15. Hitoy Cerere
16. Isla Bolaños
17. Isla del Caño
18. Isla del Coco
19. Islas Guayabo, Negritos y de los Pájaros
20. Juan Castro Blanco
21. Las Baulas
22. Lomas Barbudal
23. Manuel Antonio
24. Ostional
25. Palo Verde
26. Parque Inter. la Amistad y Chirripó
27. Peñas Blancas
28. Rincón de la Vieja
29. Santa Rosa y Guanacaste
30. Tapantí
31. Volcán Irazú
32. Volcán Póas

LOCALIZATION

Costa Rica is located in Central America, in the strip of land known as the Central American Isthmus. It borders Nicaragua in the North, Panama in the Southeast; the Pacific Ocean bathes the southern and western coastlines, and the Caribbean Sea bathes the north and northeastern coasts.

According to universal geographical coordinates, Costa Rica is located in the Northern Hemisphere to the Earth's Equator, between 8°02'26" North and 11°13'48" North and the western Hemisphere, at 82°33'48" West of Greenwich.

One of the most popular national parks in the Costa Rican Caribbean, is the Cahuita National Park, in the southern part of the basin.

CLIMATE

Costa Rica enjoys truly privileged weather. Its territorial conformation and complex topography, along with coastlines bathed by the Ocean Pacific and the Caribbean Sea, endow the Costa Rican territory with very different climates.

Due to the fact that it is a tropical country, two very well defined seasons are easy to distinguish: the dry and wet seasons; although their respective starting dates are not always predictable. The dry season happens during the months of December through April, approximately, and the rainy season goes from May to November, although it isn't strange to enjoy dry spells right in the middle of the rainy season and isolated showers during the dry season.

Exhuberant vegetation, in the Monteverde Cloud Forest Biological Reserve.

Oncidium Orchid. A very common species in the Costa Rican territory.

Fruit of the wild pineapple, a very thorny plant.

The Guanacaste area in the northeast has the most predictable weather concerning the arrival of the seasons and it is the driest, as well. The Pacific coastal area is the warmest in the country. The Caribbean area enjoys a short, dry season between September and October, although with a yearly average of 3000 to 4500 mm, it is also the most unpredictable, when it comes to predicting the weather there.

Group of individuals of the Piche species, in the lagoons and swampy zones of the Palo Verde National Park, Guanacaste.

Sunny day in the city of San José, in the quarter of Amón.

The temperature throughout the country is quite variable. It can go from between 0 °C to 15 °C in the highest mountains during the dry season. But in the Central Plateau, where most of the inhabitants have their home, the climate is very pleasant, with temperatures ranging from 19 °C to about 23 °C almost all year long. In general, the visitor considers the temperatures very pleasurable and delightful throughout the year, in spite of the humidity caused by the intense rains in the wet season.

Colourful bromeliad in one of the country's forests.

Sabre-wing hummingbird that dwells in the Rincón de la Vieja area.

GEOGRAPHY

Costa Rica possesses a great number of rivers, which irrigate all of the country's plains and valleys as they flow all the way from the mountains down to both oceans' coasts. It is also a country of many volcanoes, some of which are still active, such as Arenal, Poás, Irazú, and Rincón de la Vieja. The Costa Rican volcanic mountain ranges are independently set from other mountain ranges in Central America.

The Costa Rican mountain ranges are divided into three great groups: The Guanacaste Mountain Range, to the northeast; the Central Volcanic Range in the central part of the country, the country's largest cities lie at the foot of this mountain range; and finally the Talamanca Mountain Range, which runs towards the South and has the country's highest peaks.

Costa Rica has numerous small islands located quite near the coasts, with the exception of Cocos Island, located in the Pacific Ocean, 500 Kms from continental Costa Rican territory. Cocos Island is very famous for its legends of fabulous pirate treasures buried there by corsairs of olden times. The real treasure, nevertheless, is not buried there, it is in full view of everyone: the unspoiled, pristine state of the exuberant vegetation areas and the lush flora and fauna.

White waters of the Savegre river, south of San Gerardo of Dota.

Nymphalidae butterfly, posing on the leaf of a wild plant.

Climbing up Chirripó mountain, Talamanca Range.

Columnea bloom, widely found wild plant.

The flag of the republic of Costa Rica, flying in front of the Justice tribunals, San José.

Politics and economy

POLITICS

As a democratic country, a president, head of the government and of the State and holding the executive power, governs Costa Rica. The vice-presidents and the Cabinet assist the president in each of the government's dependencies.

Every four years, elections are held and the representatives are changed in both the executive power as well as in the legislative body. The electoral process has always been undertaken in festive spirit, characterised by the massive flying of the colourful flags, the cars noisily parading up and down the streets -filled with sympathisers-, and the so-called Plazas Públicas (public meets), where each candidate tries to convince the public that he or she is the best option there is for occupying the presidential chair.

Building of the Supreme Tribunal of Elections opposite Electoral Freedom square, San José.

Costa Rica is ruled according to a political constitution established in 1949 after the civil war. The country's powers are clearly divided into three: the executive power, the judicial power, and the legislative power. The latter is the congress and is also known as "Asamblea Legislativa". It is conformed by 57 "diputados" (deputies), elected by the people from amongst the various political parties and they are in charge of creating and modifying the law.

Costa Rica's division structure is based on a system that has seven provinces which, in turn, are divided into cantons, political units ruled by a "Municipalidad" (Municipality). The cantons are sub-divided into Districts. Costa Rica's seven provinces are: Cartago, San José, Alajuela, Heredia, Puntarenas, Guanacaste and Limón.

Morazán Park located in the heart of the city of San José.

The 'Blue Castle', near the National square, San José.

Independence celebration of Costa Rica, every 15th September.

Panoramic View of the city of San José at dawn.

Small exhibit of national agricultural produce grown in the country.

ECONOMY

Ever since its beginnings, Costa Rica has been a country of agricultural vocation and during the period between the Colony and the first half of the XIX Century, the country subsisted and provided for itself and by itself with very basic agricultural products, such as corn, which meant that everyone lived a life of scarcity and squalor then.

With the arrival of the coffee plants and the first coffee exports to Europe, Costa Rica discovered there was a better alternative for development. This in turn catapulted its economy to a much more favourable stance.

Later on, other products joined coffee, products that have now become icons in the country's economy: bananas, sugar cane, and cacao.

2nd street, San José. In the background the old building of the Costa Rica Post and Telegraph Service.

By the mid-nineteen eighties, the country's economy entered a new stage. Production of new products was incremented and this gave way to new exports, this time, of non-traditional products, such as flowers, ferns, ornamental plants, pineapples, mangos, and other tropical fruits. The production and exports of such non-traditional products generated a great deal of income and it became one of the cornerstones of the economy, as by then traditional production, mainly of coffee and bananas, began its long descent into a grave crisis, provoked by the low prices and offer excess in the world's markets.

Amistad Bridge, very important for the Guanacaste economy it joins the Nicoya peninsula with the rest of the country.

Banana plant and its still unripe fruit.

Mangos produced mainly for export to the USA and Europe.

Papaya cultivated in the warm parts of the country.

Cruise ships docking at Puntarenas pier.

More recently, and along with this increase in non-traditional agricultural exploitation, financial sectors have experienced quite a remarkable revolution through tourism and a great increment in technological production, technology that is being exported to many parts of the world.

What coffee once meant to the Costa Rican economy, is now represented by tourism. As of the end of the decade of the 90's, the hotel infrastructure and all the other platforms of offer and attention in tourism, otherwise known as "industries without chimneys", has grown continuously, to the point of becoming the greatest economic activity in the country,

Tourism in Coco beach at dusk, Guanacaste.

making Costa Rica one of the most important tourist destinations in the whole world. This has also been possible thanks to the intense and constant campaigns geared at letting the country's natural tourist attractions be known to the world at large. Along with all this increment, the country has succeeded in attracting many technology-oriented businesses that have found fertile ground and most conveniently, the necessary logistics to start their production plants in the country, giving a strong, forward push to the economy. Such is the case of the American company INTEL, which has been based in Costa Rica since the decade of the 90's and has become one of Costa Rica's greatest economic allies, due to the magnitude of their exports.

Group of tourists practicing rafting in the white waters of Pacuare river.

Production of tropical flowers, in this case heliconias.

Natural spot to enjoy oneself in Rincón of the Vieja National Park.

View of one of the halls in the Museum of pre-Columbian Gold, San José.

History

PRE-COLOMBIAN PERIOD

Before the Spanish conquest and colonisation, small tribes inhabited the areas now occupied by the country's territory, they were settled in dispersed, unorganised hamlets and were totally unlike the Mexican or Peruvian cultures, both in their size or cultural development.

Groups or areas of different cultural influences originated or were settled here precisely because of their small proportions, and due to the fact that the land was the passageway used by both great cultures of North America, the Mesoamericans, the Mayans and the Aztecs, and those cultures of the South. On one side, there was the Mesoamerican area of influence and on the other, the area under South American influence.

The Mesoamerican influence region went from what today is known as Mexico, to the south, all the way to the Gulf of Nicoya, where this influence finally settled. Most of the inhabitants of this territory northeast of the country, known as the Chorotega, descend from aborigines who came here, running away from Olmec domination.

One of the hundreds of gold figures in the Museum of pre-Columbian Gold, San José.

On the other side, the South American influence covered the Caribbean Basin, the southern Pacific Coast and the Central Region where groups such as the Brunca or Boruca and the Huetar developed their cultures.

These aboriginal groups maintained their very own features concerning language, traditions, arts and crafts, their political organisation, their agricultural activities, their dress, and their religious beliefs. Among them, the Chorotegas stand out because of their remarkable cultural development.

Small, disperse groups of some of these ancient peoples still survive around the country today. Of their ancient population centres, one of the most representative archaeological sites is the Guayabo National Monument, located in the National Park of the same name, in the province of Cartago, to the northeast of the city of Turrialba. There, the tourists can observe ancient roadways, bridges, water reservoirs, and working aqueducts

Jade Figure, Jade Museum, San José.

National Museum, located South of the Legislative Assembly building, San José.

Gold figures, showing their usage, National Museum.

Artisan's craft with indigenous techniques and motifs in Guaitil, Guanacaste.

Mythical sphere of pre-Columbian confection, Palmar Norte.

Guayabo National Monument located on the outskirts of Turrialba volcano, Cartago.

Pre-Columbian archaeological Ruins, National Monument Guayabo.

Ruins of the church of Ujarrás, one of the last vestiges of the colonial period, Cartago.

THE COLONY

The Spanish discovered the territory that Costa Rica occupies today on 18th September 1502, when in his fourth and last voyage, Admiral Christopher Columbus disembarked and christened the island we know today as “La Uvita” with the name of “La Huerta” (The Orchard), located in the waters right opposite the port of Limón City.

In the first years, after the arrival of the Spanish, during the period that we know as the “first stage of the conquest”, Andres Niño and Gil Gonzalez Davila explored both coastlines, but they did not venture into territory which meant they had very little contact with the aborigines. In 1561, the second stage of the conquest initiates; Juan de Caballón enters the territory, thus initiating the process of disarticulation of the aboriginal societies, eliminating the Caciques´ (tribal chiefs´) leadership.

Juan Vasquez de Coronado founded the city of Cartago, the main Spanish settlement during the colonial period, in the Valley of "El Guarco" in 1562. At the same time, Vasquez de Coronado was proclaimed governor of the province of Costa Rica, after a first attempt at founding an earlier settlement in the Central Valley, the one called "Villa de Garcimuñoz", which had been attempted but without any lasting success.

From Cartago, the colonialist expansion was initiated, venturing into the territory as a whole, with the exception of the villages in the Caribbean plains, because the militaristic habits of the locals troubled the Spaniards' advances, as well as that of their Christian ideals.

In the following years, and due to the scarce number of aborigines inhabiting the land, and to not finding any gold, at least in quantities that created a real interest for the Europeans and also because its main settlement was located well within the country's interior, this particular colony remained almost forgotten by the Spanish Crown. The colonists who did stay in this province were forced to turn to doing the farm work themselves in order to be able to subsist, a very different panorama from that of the neighbouring Central American countries, where a great process exploitation of the resources, and massive use of cheap aboriginal handwork were always implemented.

Baking homemade bread. Tradition introduced since the colonial period and very popular even nowadays.

Colonial Church of San Blas, located in the centre of the city of Nicoya.

RECENT HISTORY

As soon as it became independent in 1821, Costa Rica started to develop its own identity, politically as well as culturally, without any great social happenings. Nevertheless, in 1856 the American adventurer and mercenary William Walker invaded from the north, entering our country by crossing the border with Nicaragua with the firm purpose in his mind of conquering all of Central America and forcing its inhabitants into slavery. With such a threat before it, this country organised its citizens into an informal but brave and effective army led by the current president of the republic himself, Juan Rafael Mora, and after two ferocious battles, one in the Hacienda de Santa Rosa (Santa Rosa Manor), near Liberia in Guanacaste and the next in the town of Rivas in Nicaragua, the mercenary was finally expelled from the region, not having achieved his treacherous goal.

Inside view of Hacienda Santa Rosa Manor, Santa Rosa National Park.

Central park in the "White City", Liberia, Guanacaste.

Right after the episode in which these historic events took place, the country started to really develop its own democratic culture, the Costa Ricans' true pride and joy nowadays. In spite of some delays and power struggles at the time, the right to vote was finally established and primary education was declared "gratuitous and obligatory". Also, the country's economy started to really take off with the first exports to Europe, of coffee, to name the most important.

With the money that started to pour in from Europe thanks to these exports, the building of the precious neo-classic style National Theatre was undertaken and it was finally inaugurated in 1897, along with some other beautiful buildings in the city of San José, of which only few still remain, mainly in "Barrio Dent".

The period between 1940 and 1950 turned out to be crucial for this country, and at the same time it left quite a lesson for the Costa Rican people. First, a complete social reform was implemented which would come to benefit the working class of the country as a whole, as well as the creation of health services for all inhabitants, all of which was the doing of then President don Rafael Ángel Calderón Guardia. Nevertheless, in 1948, civil war broke out due to the government's refusal to acknowledge the victory of candidate Otilio Ulate Blanco, elected by the people's free vote, but belonged to the party of the opposition.

The National Square with the National Monument, San José.

Detailed façade of the old building of Post and Telegraphs of Costa Rica, San José.

It is here and now that the figure of José Figueres Ferrer enters the political scene during these events, the man who led the revolution against the government, looking for a way to enforce the choice the people had actually made. Thus it was that after several weeks of intense fighting, José Figueres Ferrer finally took over power, only to surrender it to the people's will and their choice, Otilio Ulate Blanco, the man who had actually won the elections.

As a positive result, this revolution left the people and the country a new political constitution, which is legitimate to-date, and it also caused the complete abolition of the army.

After the events of 1948, the country went on to consolidate itself as a true democracy, currently acknowledged as an example to the whole wide world.

Hospital Calderón Guardia, its name in honour of the ex-president of the Republic, San José.

Church of la Merced located in front of the park of the same name, San José.

People and culture

Fans merrily supporting the National Football Team.

THE COSTA RICANS

"Ticos", as Costa Ricans are known, are very peace loving people, contented and hospitable by nature. It is only natural to see people everywhere smiling all the time. Ticos like to show their country off, their towns and their traditions and feel very proud of what they are.

These features of Ticos are not casual, as they are people with a really solid democratic tradition and they do not have an army, the institution was abolished in 1948. Another characteristic of this society is the little social tension there is amongst its inhabitants, since, unlike other underdeveloped countries, in Costa Rica there is a large middle class, the higher and lower classes being minorities. This feature has deterred the proliferation of any extremist groups amongst the inhabitants and each and every Costa Rican feels an equal to his fellow neighbour, no more no less

Crowded and colourful bullfight, 'the Tico way', Liberia.

Children of Cañas resting after taking part in a parade around the city, Guanacaste.

Beautiful specimen and its rider, participating in a horse parade, Liberia.

We are talking here about people filled with hope, peace-loving people who have deep faith in the future, people who work really hard so that their children will be able to study and become professionals and get ahead in life. As a token, we can mention the fact that in Costa Rica, education was declared gratuitous and obligatory for all citizens in 1869, opening the door of knowledge to all social classes.

Ticos truly believe in education being the most successful means to achieve true personal development and to effectively enforce the nation's development. Currently, the average educational level of the population is comparable to that of some more highly-developed countries

Making typical tortillas by hand in Santa Cruz, Guanacaste.

Tourists taking photographs in front of the building known as "Escuela Metálica", San José.

Culture Plaza, a meeting place in the city of San José.

Students in the famous "pretil" (sitting area) of the University of Costa Rica, San José .

Museum of the Children, a former penitentiary which now houses this museum, San José.

CULTURE

The cultural conceptualisation of Costa Rica starts back in pre-Columbian times, when aborigines cultivated native crops such as corn, which is still part of any modern-day Tico's diet. But the biggest cultural influence came from Europe, with the arrival of the Spanish conquistadors. As examples, we shall mention Spanish, the country's official language; the architecture, the influence in the design and location of catholic temples is quite obvious; the political system, with its long lasting democratic regime; the country's main religion, Catholicism -introduced by the Spaniards- is still the country's official religion; the food with its many different styles combines the last vestiges of Spanish "fogones" with traces of the aboriginal diet which have got so much better with the times, conforming itself to the intercultural winds, making it more dynamic and giving Costa Rican cuisine a very particular flavour.

It is important to mention that throughout the last centuries, Costa Rica has seen the arrival of important numbers of immigrants who have made their contributions into Costa Rica's unique culture. Such is the case of the European immigrants, during the two world wars, earlier were the Jamaicans and their influence all along the Caribbean coast, and in the last decades, the Nicaraguans, who have incorporated themselves, in massive quantities, into the country's cheap labour infrastructure.

Typical red taxis circulating opposite the Church of La Soledad, San José.

Colourful and detailed wheel of the emblematic, typical ox cart .

Fountain of the Hispanidad at the beginning of the night, in San Pedro, to the east of the city of San José.

Nevertheless, the most important source of cultural influence comes from the north, from the United States of America. It is logical to think that because of our proximity to this world power, and due to our commercial affairs, there is currently a great deal of American influence, which can be seen in the extended use of English as a second language, in the proliferation of the great shopping centres, the "Malls", the tendencies in the ways in which Ticos dress, the influence that comes through television, the irruption of the concept of fast food or junk food

and, yes, the influence in almost all areas of the country and the people's daily life, which have been assimilated in the course of time and are clearly of American origin.

This melting pot of foreign influences come during the course of many years, along with the Costa Ricans' particular ways and habits, have turned Costa Rica and Ticos into quite a unique mixture in the continent.

The nature

Boat transiting one of the canals of the Tortuguero National Park, Limón.

THE ECOSYSTEMS

Due to its privileged geographical position, and because of its natural biological conditions, Costa Rica presents a great variety of terrestrial and maritime ecosystems, and salt water and fresh water marshlands.

In the country, different ecological classification criteria are used, nevertheless, the one with the best adaptation to national reality is the one that groups the ecosystems based on their particular characteristics, they are divided into: Forests, wetlands, and marine and agricultural ecosystems.

One of the greatest attractions for visitors to this land is in fact the amazing variety of the Ecosystems and the great biodiversity that they harbour, in a country traditionally mindful of the preservation of nature and of the environment, and which has actively participated in many programmes of conservation.

Beautiful bloom of the Trichopilia Orchid.

Butterfly Nymphalidae, displaying its wings, gracefully spotted with geometrical forms.

Mist in the forest of the basin of the Savegre river, Llano Azúl.

FOREST ECOSYSTEMS

A great extension of the Costa Rican territory is covered by forests, some of which have been protected forever and ever by laws pursued by people who are completely committed to the preservation of the environment and incrementally supported by government and private efforts advocated to this cause. The country's great challenge will be to achieve the complete preservation of at least these forests, which currently cover 35% of the national territory. The Costa Rican forests are classified into: Tropical rainforests, cloud forests, lowland cloud forests, and mangrove forests, with this last type being the most extensive

The forested ecosystems are distributed practically all over the country.

Basilisk, very common in the margins of the rivers and lagoons of the north of the country.

The lagoon of Caño Negro, in the plains of the North, reaches its biggest size in the months of rain.

WETLANDS

In recent times, the wetlands have become objects of great relevance for communities and organisations interested in the conservation of nature. Costa Rica is one of the countries that have shown the greatest interest in its own ecosystems, and many of its wetlands have been declared Wetlands of International Importance, also known as the Ramsar sites.

This category also includes other ecosystems of great importance to mankind, such as mangrove forests, estuaries, and other sites, all associated to the sea.

Concerning freshwater ecosystems, we can mention places such as several different lakes, lagoons and various marshes.

MARINE ECOSYSTEMS

This category, predominantly made up of coral reef platforms, has great ecological importance as many marine species only reproduce in these particular niches. They are of great importance to mankind as well, since a great deal of the seafood and fish that are consumed, come from these particular areas.

Costa Rica has coral reefs on both coasts, the largest ones are found just off the southern Caribbean coast.

Currently, these ecosystems are in great danger of disappearing due to over exploitation of their resources, the pollution in the rivers that flow into the coastal seawater and the damage produced by direct contamination of the sites, all of which, represents a constant threat to the delicate balance of such ecosystems.

Lora turtles, leaving to the sea after spawning on Ostional beach, Guanacaste.

Fishermen picking up their fishnets in Puerto Viejo, Limón.

Fishermen sporting the fruits of their labour, Cahuita Limón.

Flower of Pachira, its size in full bloom reaches 40 cm or more.

Biodiversity

If there is anything the Costa Rican people can be proud of, it is the great biodiversity the Costa Rican territory harbours, because no other country in the world has anything like it, when compared to the proportional size of the country, it is the greatest ever reported. In fact, it is considered that Costa Rica is the country with the largest amount of living species per square kilometre on Planet Earth.

Within its 51 0002 kilometres, the equivalent of just 0,01% of the Earth's surface, Costa Rica houses an amazing 4% of all the world's living species.

It is has been calculated that in Costa Rica, there are about 500,000 species, of which only 18% of them have ever been officially described. This is due to the fact that the largest group is the arthropod group and only 20% of the total amounts of species have ever been described. The second group in importance by size is the plant group.

Nymphalidae Butterfly, resting on the green foliage.

The most consistently described group, in which 98.9% of its species are known, is that of the terrestrial vertebrates. At the other end of the line, are the invertebrates, the less known group, as 98% of these creatures are still waiting for their official discovery.

The huge biodiversity that we can find in its many ecosystems, make Costa Rica the ideal paradise for natural scholars and ecology enthusiasts and conservationists.

Heliconia after blooming, it keeps its intense yellow colour.

Group of seagulls, flying and scanning the beach in search of food.

Iguana sunbathing, one of the most common reptiles in Costa Rica.

Poisonous Oropel serpent, its intense colour warns predators.

FAUNA

Honouring the country's reputation as one among those with the greatest biodiversity, a considerable amount of fauna come from the exchange between the northern part and southern part of the American continent has managed to settle into this narrow land, allowing for the chance to register monkey species from South America along with felines from North America, for instance.

Due to its geographical position, its topography and its climate, Costa Rica is able to lodge mammals along with birds, amphibians, and insects which have adapted to the diverse conditions, from jungles to urban centres.

It really must be said in all truth that the current conservation effort of the local fauna and its preservation for generations to come has been achieved thanks to the creation of National Parks and National Reserves of all kinds, which have been able to incorporate the greatest quantity of fauna within their limits.

The red-eyed arboreal frog, is a species of nocturnal habits.

The hummingbirds are a big group within the 840 bird species that inhabit the country.

Mammals

It is believed that more than 260 species of mammals, both marine and terrestrial, exist inside the area that the country occupies. Some of them can be easily observed from the roadsides when travelling around the country's many different routes. Among them we can mention howler monkeys, and "coatis". Nevertheless, if you want to see some of the less common species, it is necessary to keep an open eye for them, especially inside of the limits of the different parks which can be visited. Most of the mammals that inhabit the land are bats, of which there are more than 200 species; but in this particular work we shall concentrate on other, more visually attractive species.

• **The Feline Family:** Without a doubt, hearing the roar of the great Jaguar in the deep forest is one of the most incredible experiences for anyone. This great feline, the greatest in Central America, shares its territory with five smaller sized felines, among them the Puma.

• **Monkeys:** They all belong to the Cebidae family. All four monkey species that inhabit this land, are fairly common, and are easy to spot, if you go to the right location:

The sloth is a mammal that lives in the treetops.

Howler monkey eating leaves in the treetop.

The Howler monkey, also known as Congo monkey is the biggest of all four species. Its name comes from the loud howl the male monkeys emit, which creates the sensation of belonging to a much larger animal so large it can be heard from hundreds of metres away. Practically black in colour, this loud monkey likes living in the trees, usually in familial groups of about 10 individuals. It is common to see them in the secondary forests near urban centres and, at times, right there in the trees of many hotel gardens.

White faced monkeys are curious before the camera.

The smallest specimens are called Titi monkeys. This rare species which inhabits the Central and South Pacific, is in danger of extinction, due mainly to the destruction of its natural habitat and because, due to its attractive dimensions, unscrupulous people see them as delectable pets. They generally come with golden-brown fur and a long prehensile tail. It can be observed in Manuel Antonio National Park, looking for fruit and insects among the tree branches.

The "Carablanca" (White Face), so called because of the white fur on the front part of its head while the rest of its body is pitch black. Despite the fact that it is more widely spread than the Titi, it is common to see both species dwelling together in some places.

Mother Titi protecting and carrying its small offspring on its back.

Lastly, we shall mention the Spider Monkey; this one prefers the rainforests and cloud forests located along the Pacific Coast. Its long limbs allow it to be a great acrobat, a virtue which can be appreciated in the grace and agility with which it moves from one branch to another high up in the tall trees.

Other important groups of mammals that inhabit the different regions of Costa Rica are the anteaters, opossums, sloths, raccoons, and rodents.

Honey bear in search of food.

Agouti walking on the beach.

Pizote or coati, with its enormous tail almost as long as its whole body and totally erect.

Birds

Many birdwatchers from all over the world come to this small country with the hope of being able to watch the great numbers of tropical birds in their natural habitat, within relatively small extensions of land. More than 840 species of birds have been registered, most of them permanent residents.

Perhaps the most attractive characteristic of the birds that live in the tropics, is their magnificent, resplendent and colourful plumage and, in the mating season, the melodious chords of their birdsong.

"Candelita collareja" exhibiting its dramatic colours.

Mirlo (blackbird) resting on a branch in the highlands.

Parrots like the beautiful, colourful "Red Macaw", which can be seen with its spectacular plumage adorning the national parks of Corcovado and Carara in the Pacific, represent one of the tourists' most attractive birds to watch.

But the hummingbird, a bird species that only exists in the American continent, and has more than 50 different species all over the territory, is another very interesting bird group for tourists to watch.

They can be admired in great quantities in private feeding grounds or in any garden for that matter.

The famous Trogons, birds of beautifully coloured plumage, count the magnificent Quetzal among their ranks, a real trophy for any birdwatcher. This bird has been deeply admired since times of old in the entire Central American region. Even though this colourful bird, with a tail over 50 centimetres long, and white, crimson and iridescent-emerald-green feathers is not easy to find, it is possible to see it when feeding on "aguacatillos", the fruit of the wild mountain avocado tree –its favourite treat.

On both, the Pacific Ocean and Caribbean Sea coasts, one can see a great variety of wild waterfowl, known as "playeros" (beach birds). There are several different families that can be easily spotted on tourist beaches, many of them in great flocks, looking for food and flying back to their nests at dusk.

The resplendent quetzal is one of the most colourful birds in the country, it lives in the mountains.

The Caracará is a bird of prey of strong beak.

Quail spends a great deal of its time looking for food on the forest ground.

The Reinita Mielera (Little Honey Queen) extracts the nectar from the flowers with its fine beak.

Woodpecker at the entrance of its nest.

The Spoonbill can be observed on the riverbanks and lakes.

Lora Turtle in Nancite beach after laying eggs.

Reptiles

Among the most interesting reptiles for tourists to see, because of their great size and massive arrivals on the beaches, are the sea turtles, which visit both coastlines of the country.

In the second semester of each year, it is very common to see the arrival of hundreds of turtles, which, in a matter of only a few hours, come to lay their eggs on beaches such as Ostional Beach, in the peninsula of Guanacaste, on the Pacific coast. In many cases, you can see how the little newborn turtles, as they hatch, take swiftly to the sea, while at the same time their adult counterparts, hundreds of times bigger, diligently try to find a safe spot to lay their eggs on the beach, as far away from predators as possible.

The easiest reptiles to spot and enjoy are the lizards and the iguanas, despite the fact that serpents count for more than half of all the reptiles in Costa Rica. This is due to the fact that snakes are extremely shy, which makes them hard to spot.

The green iguana and the “garrobo” are the most common; they are easy to spot on beaches, riverbanks and other sometimes really unexpected places!

The striking green basilisk lizard is quite the show, not only because of its dashing bright-green-coloured coat but also because it can be seen –quite literally, dashing across the water, on the surfaces of rivers, lagoons and ponds.

Caimans and crocodiles are fairly common in quite a few places. The former can be found in many of the country’s rivers, wetlands and lagoons. Crocodiles, though, are a bit more scarce, despite the fact that they are very easy to spot on the banks of the Tárcoles River mouth, on the central Pacific coast

Green Spiny Lizard sunbathing.

Cayman disguising itself on the bottom of this lagoon.

Boa serpent rolled up on the dead leaves.

The red poisonous frog is a variety of the type of frogs called spearheads.

Amphibians

Frogs are the most striking of all. They are found in a great variety of colours and sizes, and in many different habitats. The Arrowhead frog can be seen with different colour coats. Not all of these species are poisonous, although some may secrete a very toxic kind of venom. In the old days, the aborigines of these lands utilised this venom on their arrowheads, hence their name.

A particularly curious species of Arrowhead frog, sports a fiery red colour on its body and a deep blue colour on its hind limbs, making it look as if it were wearing blue jeans.

The green black poisonous spearhead frog, warns predators with its colours.

The MORPHO butterfly is known for its blue coloured wings.

Insects

This group is the most varied and numerous. It has been determined that specimens of 10% of all the planet's living insects can be found in this country.

The most striking of all are the butterflies. It has been estimated that they make up for more than 560 species, with the Morphs and their impressive colours being the most outstanding. The common Great Blue butterfly is one of these species; they are easily seen in many forests and national parks, fluttering among the greenery, contrasting with their gorgeous, glistening metallic light blue wings.

Ants are very common in all of the world's tropical rainforests and Costa Rica is no exception. It is easy to find leaf-cutting ants marching untiringly on the jungle floor, following the trail they had opened themselves to commute from their underground chambers to the food-collection spots. They can be seen carrying leaves' fragments, enormous in proportion to their own dimensions. The leaves are not really their food; instead they are the raw material to cultivate a kind of fungus that is later turned into their source of sustenance. Also, depending on the area where we are located, it is easy to find shepherd ants, bullet Ants that have a very painful bite which can cause great swelling and even a fever.

Mariquita (ladybug) common insect in the tropical forest.

Spider making its web to catch its prey.

In all regions of the country, a great variety of colourful butterflies can be seen.

Heliconius Butterfly. Although its wings are not very big, it is very colourful when flying.

Grasshopper of rare light blue eyes.

Butterfly collecting the nectar of the flowers, at the same time it pollinates the bloom.

The Guanacaste tree is officially the National Tree.

FLORA

Costa Rica's flora is not even nearly homogeneous. Due to its privileged geographical position in the continent, and the great variety of ecosystems, it presents a rather great variety of sorts. It is considered that there are more than 100 000 plant species considered superior, from the magnificent trees, -some of precious woods and in danger of extinction- to the exuberant orchids.

A local observing the birds in an oak tree.

Trees in the cloud forest of Costa Rica, with lichens and moss.

Trees

The Corteza Amarilla (Yellow Bark) trees are very common in the dry parts of the Pacific. They shed most of their leaves in the first months of every year, and then go into bloom, when a spectacular yellow efflorescence takes place and lasts for many days.

The Poró is a beautiful tree that was once used to divide estates and to give shade in the large coffee plantations. With the elimination of the coffee plantations, due to urban development, it has become ever more scarce, though it is still fairly easy to see. Its flowers can go from blood red to orange and it is in bloom in the month of February.

The Roble de Sabana (Oak of the grassy plains) is easy to find in different parts of both basins, the Pacific and Caribbean. In the Central Plateau it can be seen adorning the roads, boulevards and motorways and some parks. It is easy to spot, as it blooms copiously with its tender rosy-coloured efflorescence during the first months of the year, mainly between January and April.

Coconut grove in the Costa Rican Caribbean.

Brassia Orchid in the Lankester Botanical gardens of Cartago.

Orchids

Popular belief erroneously considers that orchids are parasite plants, but they are actually epiphytes; this means that they are guests and that they simply use trees as support, not sustenance, and they cause trees no harm. Just in Costa Rica, there are more than 1400 different species. A special place to see a great deal of these plants is the Lankester Botanical Gardens, located in Cartago. The months of February and March are ideal to go and enjoy the greatest amount of them, in bloom.

Traditionally most orchids in this country are called "Guarias". It is a word with indigenous roots: "guar", 'tree', describes an aspect of the plant's way of life. The "Guariantes" and the "Cattleyas" are the most representative of the area.

Without a doubt, the most beloved flower in Costa Rica is the Guarianthe Skinneri or Guaria Morada. This plant, with beautiful lavender or lilac blooms, also has a variety that is quite scarce, and totally white, called "Alba", which has currently brought about the creation of several groups of fans who are totally into its reproduction and care. After all, it is Costa Rica's national flower.

The bromeliads make another very common group of plants in the rainforests, with their bracts and their colourful leaves; they play an important part in the forest's life. Water collects inside of their bosom, so they are used as water fountains by many different animals that inhabit the cloud forests. Hummingbirds also visit them constantly looking for nectar, and frogs nest within their wet furrows. This is why a scientist once catalogued bromeliads as "aerial swamps". It is common to find them on tree trunks and boughs, as well as amongst mosses, lichens, and orchids.

Encyclia Orchid.

Cochleanthes Orchid, known for its nice aroma.

Regions

For practical reasons, in this publication we have used a way of dividing the country into regions which has taken us touring around the different locations, those of greatest interest to the tourist, and also the most charming ones in the country: the Central Plateau, the Northeast, the Central Pacific, the Caribbean, and the South.

Vista of the Central Square of San José, towards the east.

CENTRAL PLATEAU

Set right in the country's heart, the Central Plateau or Central Valley, as it is also known, covers an extension of a little over 1500 Kms2. It limits with the Central Mountain Range to the North, where the impressive Irazú and Poás volcanoes are located; to the South, by the northern tip of the Talamanca Mountain Range; to the East, extending itself all the way to Paraíso, in Cartago, and to the west all the way to San Ramón, in Alajuela.

The largest urban centres in the country are located in the Central Plateau; this area houses more than 40% of the Costa Rican population, it is distributed in and around the province capitals and some important cantonal capitals as well. The cities of Alajuela, Cartago, and Heredia are located within a radius of 25 Kms from the San José downtown area. This proximity allows for an urban concentration that makes it ever more difficult to identify the cities' natural limits.

Panoramic view of the city of San José, towards the south.

The Paseo Colón is the most important entranceway into San José. from the west.

Beautiful building of the Cathedral of San José.

Panoramic view that shows the National Theatre and the Square of Culture, San José.

SAN JOSÉ

Located at the heart of the Central Plateau, at a height of 1150 mts. above sea level, San José was once a humble town, all but forgotten in olden-day Central America, long after the colonial period had ended. But, given the boom of coffee exports, as of 1850, this small hamlet started to transform itself into a city with great European influence, which could be seen in the local architecture of those days and in all the Europe-imported goods there were.

Impressive inside view of the National Theatre in San José, built with funds coming from the first coffee exports and inaugurated in 1897.

National Culture Centre, formerly the building of the National Liquor Factory, San José.

A living symbol of the architecture of the time and the pride of all Central America is the National Theatre. This beautiful work of architectural art was inaugurated in 1897, with the presentation of the opera Faust. After the completion of the Theatre, which looked so imposing amidst the small adobe houses and cobble stone streets, San José began to transform itself gradually, to the point where it became a lively, cosmopolitan city.

Currently, San José no longer has many of its old-day buildings, although if you walk around the city, you will probably find some samples of the charming architecture of the last century.

As in almost all the cities in Costa Rica, San José is a city structured into small square blocks where people are in the habit of strolling up and down the city and the parks.

La Sabana Park, place of recreation for many josefinos.

Group of tourists walking down the city of San José.

A common day in the crowded Central Avenue, San José.

ALAJUELA

Located in the western part of the Central Valley, it is the main gateway of entrance into the country, since this province houses the international airport. It is the second city in size, after the capital, San José.

Very close to this city, and also belonging to this province, are places with great touristic importance: Poás Volcano, with its impressive crater, easily accessible by car; the town of Zarcero and its gorgeous park, with its famous natural plant sculptures; the Artisan's Centre in Sarchí, considered one of the country's most representative, because of the artisans' way of treating of the precious woods, in addition to the colourful designs of the typical oxcarts; we will not forget to mention the beautiful surroundings of the Alajuela countryside.

The Poás Volcano National Park is one of the most assiduously visited places by both national and foreign tourists. It has an extension of 6.500 hectares and it is a place of great natural and scenic beauty. It is an active volcano of sub conic shape, with a crater of enormous dimensions, considered one of the largest in the whole world.

Zarcero square, famous for its natural sculptures, Alajuela.

Tourists observing the crater in Poás Volcano National Park.

The lagoon of Botos formerly a crater, Poás volcano.

Artisan of Sarchí painting the wheel of the typical oxcart, Alajuela.

Basílica of 'Nuestra Señora de los Ángeles' in the city of Cartago.

CARTAGO

Located at the eastern end of the Central Plateau, Cartago, capital of Costa Rica until 1823, when it was definitely moved to San José. At an altitude of 1400 mts above sea level, Cartago has the coolest climate among the main cities of the Central Plateau. Guarded from the North by the impressive Irazú Volcano, Cartago is the third city in population density.

For Costa Ricans, Cartago has a special charm, and it is that this city is the home of the holy Virgin of The Angels, better known as "La Negrita", which Costa Rican Catholics venerate as their patron saint. The Catholic religion is the most widespread in Costa Rica, and thus, every year, hundreds of thousands of pilgrims walk massively to visit their patron saint's shrine, in Cartago, to see her on 2nd August of every year.

Irazú Volcano is Cartago's great natural tourist attraction, it can be visited and people can enjoy the surrounding scenery, with beautiful fields, and picturesque little towns. The valley of Orosi lies more to the east, again, with great scenic beauty and crisscrossed by beautiful, pristine rivers, it is a must-see. There are two gorgeous colonial churches there, Ujarrás, currently in ruins, and the Church of Orosi with its small museum of colonial religious art.

If it is nature you wanted to talk about, to the east of this valley is the Tapantí Wildlife Refuge, one of the region's rainiest forests, with its exuberant vegetation.

Two impressive rivers cross this region: the Reventazón, and the Pacuare, both are considered white-water rivers and are very popular for the practice of rafting and kayaking.

Ruins of the church of Santiago in the centre of the city of Cartago.

Crater of the Irazú volcano, located to the north of Cartago.

Pejibayes in the Central Market of Cartago.

Colonial church of Orosi and its gardens.

Bloom of the Guaria Turrialba, in the Lankester Botanical Garden, Cartago.

Strawberries cultivated in Heredia.

HEREDIA

Located 11 kms North of San José, at 1150 mts above sea level, the city of Heredia boasts a cool climate and its surrounding, extensive coffee plantations. Its beautiful countryside is widely visited, mainly to the North of the city, where the hills are still filled with cypress forests, as well as green pasturelands. The Univeridad Nacional important centre of superior studies in Costa Rica is located downtown, in Heredia. Next to the Municipal Palace is the interesting historic site of "El Fortín" (the Turret). 3 kms to the North of the city centre, is the town of Barva, where the park is surrounded by the old adobe houses, and a gorgeous white stucco church, all very Old Spanish, in style.

More to the North, on the way to Puerto Viejo de Sarapiquí, we find a series of impressive waterfalls, called La Paz , they are set amidst a lush cloud forest.

The Fortín (turret), colonial vestige in the city of Heredia.

Wild bloom awaiting its natural pollinator.

Waterfall of La Paz, surrounded by exuberant forest.

Female of Indigo Sabre Wing Hummingbird, shaking its wings at great speed.

Leave-cutting ants carrying a piece of a leave, Braulio Carrillo National Park.

Northwest and Nicoya peninsula

This region goes from the Guanacaste and Tilarán mountain ranges, all the way to the Nicaraguan border, in the North, and all the lands located between these ranges and the North Pacific coast.

Town of Santa Elena at the start of the night, Puntarenas.

MONTEVERDE CLOUD FOREST BIOLOGICAL RESERVE

This Cloud Forest Biological Reserve is located 6 Kms away from the town of Santa Elena. This area is world famous because of its lush cloud forests; it is constantly visited by famous scientists who come from all over the world to study its amazing biodiversity. Apart from Monteverde, this area houses the Santa Elena Biological Reserve, The Perpetual Forest Of The Children and other smaller reserves of great importance for the study of nature.

This important conservation sanctuary has received wide world recognition, due to its invaluable contribution to the conservation of wildlife in the American tropics. More that 400 species of butterflies, 440 of birds and 100 of mammals, as well as 400 species of orchids are found among its biodiversity.

Bromeliads, very common in Monteverde.

Bridges on the tops of the trees, Monteverde.

Trees of the cloud forest, Monteverde .

Group of birdwatchers on the footpaths of Monteverde.

Monteverde Cloud Forest Biological Reserve.

The forests of Costa Rica contain the biggest diversity of flora in the whole world.

VOLCÁN TENORIO NATIONAL PARK

Located in the Guanacaste Mountain Range, It has greatly changeable weather due to the influence of weather patterns from both the Pacific and the Caribbean continental divides.

Its great attractions are the famous "Light-Blue" River (Río Celeste) with its waterfall, its steamers, and its thermal waters. Diverse minerals are mixed in the water and dye it, giving it the very particular light-blue colouration of its waters.

Curious natural coloration of the Celeste river, Tenorio Volcano.

Forest in Volcán Tenorio National Park.

Waterfall in Celeste river, cascading down into a pool of intense light blue colour.

Bromeliad with its dramatic colours, lives in the trunks and thick boughs of the trees.

RINCÓN DE LA VIEJA NATIONAL PARK

This park, located in the Guanacaste Mountain Range, 26 kms North from the city of Liberia, is famous for having the largest population of Guaria Morada orchids in the wild, and because of the areas of geological activity called Las Pailas (The Cauldrons) and las Hornillas (the Ovens). The park gets its name from the volcano of the same name, and it has a height of 1926 mts above sea level, it is currently in a stage of fumarole activity.

Tourists walking near the crater of the Rincón of the Vieja volcano.

Waterfall La Cangreja, refreshing waterfall in the vicinity of the Rincón de la Vieja.

The Rincón of the Vieja National Park is one of the last natural strongholds of the Guaria Morada, the national flower.

Cráter of the Rincón of the Vieja volcano, with its turquoise coloured lagoon.

Area of geological activity called the Pailas, Rincón of the Vieja volcano.

Old tree in the forest of Rincón of the Vieja National Park.

Panoramic view during the dry season, Palo Verde National Park.

PALO VERDE NATIONAL PARK

This is one of the parks with the most biodiversity in this country, located 28 kms from the city of Cañas; the Bebedero and Tempisque rivers surround it and frequently flood it, during the rainy season, creating the lagoons and swamps that are ideal for the survival of various species of flora and fauna, especially waterfowl, and wading birds. Some 300 species of varied waterfowl are thought to inhabit this reserve, counting both migratory and resident birds. During the months of September and March, it is common to see a great variety of species in the different habitats, in amounts that count up to the thousands; one can see birds such as herons, ibex, plunger birds, ducks, and many others.

The name of this park is owed to an almost totally green shrub that is found everywhere in the park area.

North of this national park is the Lomas de Barbudal Biological Reserve, that keeps a good sampling of tropical forest, with some species of trees in danger of extinction.

Dry Forest of the Palo Verde National Park, quite typical in the area.

Waterfall Llanos del Cortés, near Lomas de Barbudal Biological Reserve.

Sunset in Liberia, also known as the white city, due to the coloration of its dirt.

LIBERIA

Known as the White City, Liberia is located just over 200 Kms west of San José, right on the edge of the Inter American motorway. Its strategic position in the heart of Guanacaste makes this city the point of departure to the various Guanacaste beaches and national parks, north and east of the province. This city is currently growing fast; it has an international airport that now gets an ever-growing number of tourists and offers all the services of modern city life. South of Liberia's Central Park, you can visit an interesting area of really old houses, some over 150 years old.

Liberia City, Guanacaste.

Playas del Coco (Coconut beach) was for a long time the most popular swimming resort in Guanacaste.

GULF OF PAPAGAYO AND NORTH BEACHES

Considered a tourist's paradise, the gulf of Papagayo in the North of Guanacaste has recently undergone a process of great growth in high-class hotel infrastructure; many Hollywood stars and world personalities visit the luxurious hotels lodged in its hills, others have their summer residences on these beautiful beaches, or in their surroundings.

Many tourist places are located here, there are beaches everywhere; among the most famous are: El Coco, well known among surfers and for many years the favourite beach of "Josefinos" (San José city residents), who love spending their holidays there. Flamingo renowned for its clean white sands, quiet environment, top-of-the-line hotels, the great offer of sports fishing tours and sports fishing equipment. Further to the south lies the small, lively tourist town of Tamarindo, with its huge beach. It is one of Costa Rica's vacationers' favourite places, as it has all the commodities, it is ideal all year long for the practice of surfing, it has great ambiance, both in the daytime as well as in the night time, and the gorgeous beach is fit for having lots of fun.

Summer sunset in Tamarindo Beach, Guanacaste.

Practising surfing on the waves of Playas del Coco.

Flamingo Beach, in the peninsula of Guanacaste.

Life at the beach in the crowded town of Tamarindo.

Vista of the great beach of Tamarindo at dusk.

Playas del Coco on a summer day, Guanacaste.

Guanacasteca' and her intense tan under the Guanacaste sun.

Park ranger with his official uniform in the Santa Rosa National Park, Guanacaste.

The Coral snake can be found in the Santa Rosa National Park, Guanacaste.

SANTA ROSA NATIONAL PARK

Located in the north of Guanacaste, it safeguards the most important zone of dry tropical forest in all of Central America. This forest is characterised for being lush and green in the rainy season and, with the coming of the dry season, most of the trees in the whole forest become extremely dry. Among the abundant fauna that inhabits this park, important populations of jaguars and pumas are the most outstanding.

The beautiful beaches, Naranjo and Nancite, are of great relevance to the Central American region for being the favourite egg-laying sites for Leatherback and Lora turtles. From the historic point of view, Santa Rosa actually constitutes an icon of the Costa Ricans' desire to remain free; it is here that Hacienda Santa Rosa Manor house is located. This house was the site of the Battle of Santa Rosa, in March of 1856. It was here that the great 1856 feat of the victory against the American Filibuster

Panoramic view of the dry forest, towards the beach in the Santa Rosa National Park, Guanacaste.

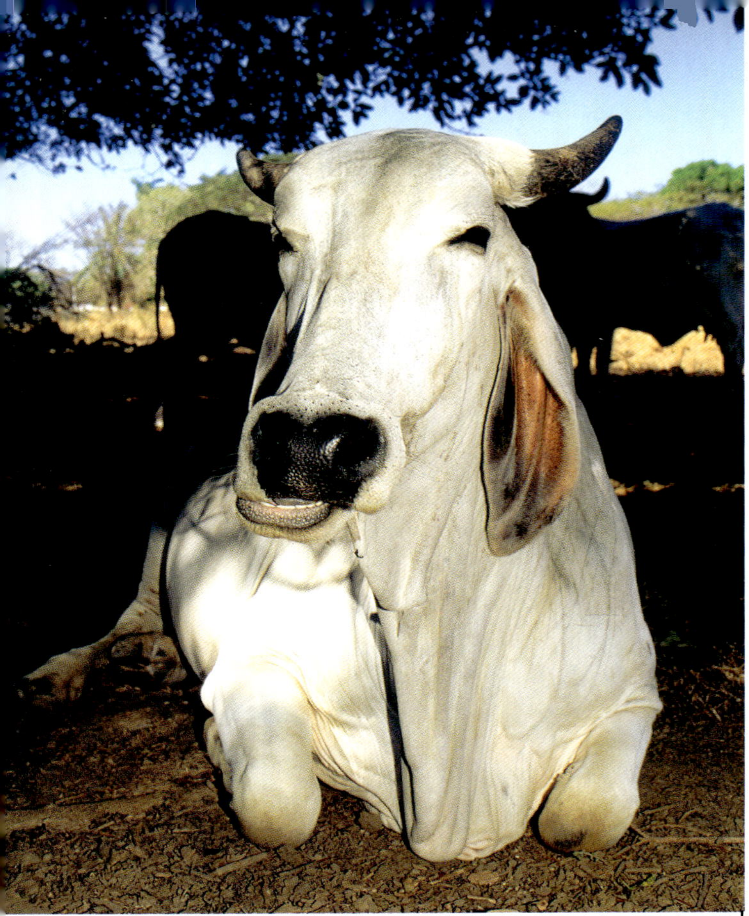

Cattle farming has diminished in Nicoya, nevertheless, it still is an important economic activity.

Vista of the city of Nicoya in the peninsula of the same name, Guanacaste.

Typical sabanero nicoyano (ranger), after a hard day's work.

NICOYA

Located in the heart of the peninsula of Nicoya, this city, owes its name to Cacique (Indian chief) Nicoya, who lived in the area in colonial times. The colonial church of San Blas, built in the middle of the XVII century, is the most representative in the city. Nicoya is not only the unavoidable point of departure to get to the central part of the province, and south, to the namesake peninsula, but it is also an important trade and business centre; even back in colonial times, great quantities of cattle and goods were commercialised there.

Carrillo Beach is famous in the peninsula of Guanacaste due to the light coloured sand and the great quantity of coconuts on the waterfront.

SÁMARA BEACH AND CARRILLO BEACH

These beaches are located on the south-western coast of the peninsula of Nicoya. Tourists love the white sand beaches, and hotel infrastructure there. Samara is located 35 Kms south of the city of Nicoya, and Carrillo, 3 Kms south of Samara. This latter beach, still quite undeveloped, is famous for the large palm trees that surround it, as well as for its unspoiled, white sands. There is a small airstrip right next to the beach.

Sámara Beach is one of the favourite destinations for tourists, Guanacaste.

Young merchant selling the typical frappes on the beach, Sámara.

Explorer inside of one of the independent caverns, in Barra Honda, Guanacaste.

Dusty road to the Barra Honda National Park, Guanacaste.

BARRA HONDA NATIONAL PARK

Located 22 kms south of Nicoya, Barra Honda is a very special place thanks to its system of independent caves, which are embedded within the several limestone peaks of coralline origin that conform it. Some of these peaks are Barra Honda, Coyol, La Cueva, and Quebrada Honda, actually, all former coral reefs that emerged to the surface. Funnily, the Barra Honda peak was thought to be a volcano, due to its shape, its grottos, and the stench produced by the guano of scores of thousands of bats that inhabit the caves. In total, 19 caverns have been explored, all belonging to different independent systems, among which we can mention La Terciopelo, La Trampa, El Perico, El Pozo y El Pozo Hediondo.

Vista from the lookout point of Barra Honda, in the summer season.

Montezuma is a great attraction for the tourists, mainly Europeans.

MONTEZUMA

Located in the southern tip of the peninsula of Nicoya, Montezuma is a picturesque beach town that belongs to the province of Puntarenas. Montezuma, along with Tamarindo and Jacó is probably the most visited beach location, sought by sun-seeking, sand-loving, relaxed-type tourists.

Montezuma has a number of very beautiful small beaches, surrounded by the most splendorous natural environment, the predominantly dry tropical forests, the cascades, ravines, and rocky areas. These features have turned this tiny place into the residence place of a great deal of foreigners, come from many different countries in the world.

Cascade in Montezuma, one of the most visited attractions in the area.

Cascade in Montezuma on the bedrock.

A walk under the sun in the principal street of the town of Montezuma.

Passengers getting off the ferry to Paquera in the península of Nicoya.

Tourists enjoying the sun and the sand on the beach of Montezuma, Península of Nicoya.

The marina in Herradura is part of the development fenomenon, on the rise in the Central Pacific.

Improvised shops in the Tourists' boulevard, Puntarenas, Central Pacific.

Central Pacific

This region is located between the Pacific coast and the various rocky formations that crisscross the country, towards the southeast, and it goes from the port-city of Puntarenas, all the way to the mouth of the Grande de Térraba River, in the south. This region houses some tourist urban centres that are very important, such as Puntarenas, Jacó, Quepos, Manuel Antonio, and Dominical, to mention the most important.

The estuary of Puntarenas is found in the north part of the city, and is very utilized by small boats.

The beach of Puntarenas is one of the most important attractions of the "Puerto".

Typical Marimba (xylophone) in the Tourists' boulevard, in the background one can see one of the enormous cruise ships that visit this pier in Puntarenas.

PUNTARENAS

This is the most important city in the Central Pacific region and it also boasts the most important Costa Rican port on the Pacific coast. It is located 130 Kms from San José. Strangely, Puntarenas was founded on a thin, long strip of sandy soil that goes quite a ways into the waters of the gulf of Nicoya.

In olden days, due to its vicinity to San José, this city was the main vacation spot for Costa Ricans, but with the passing of the years, and with the improvement of many roads, many other -further away- places began to compete with Puntarenas at attracting tourism. In spite of this, currently, "El Puerto", as it has come to be popularly called, has made quite an effort in order to maintain its competitiveness and validity. So that it currently offers an enormous beach, the cleanliness of which, is carefully kept up to standard, especially near the "Punta" (the Tip).

Puntarenas is a very lively port city that receives lots of tourists, especially at weekends and during the dry season.

Forest of Carara National Park, which is located in the Transition Area, between the dry forest and the rainforest of the coast of the Pacific Ocean.

CARARA NATIONAL PARK

This park, located at the mouth of the Grande de Tárcoles River, in the very middle of the Central Pacific area, is a Transition Zone of Dry Tropical Forest into Tropical Rainforest on the Pacific Coast.

There is a large population of American crocodiles in this park, which really calls the attention of tourists, as they can easily be seen showing off their enormous dimensions (and fangs) on the sandy riverbanks of the Grande de Tárcoles River, Carara is also a refuge for the main population of Red Macaws in the Central Pacific Coast area.

- Enormous American crocodiles in the Grande de Tárcoles River.

Carara National Park is one of the last places in the country, with an important population of red macaws.

-'Anhinga' extending its wings to dry, in the Carara National Park.

JACÓ

The small town of Jacó is the main tourist urban centre on all of the Central Pacific area. It is located near the Costanera Sur (South Coast) road, which, as its name clearly indicates, runs along the South Pacific area, parallel with the coastline. Its beach is 4 Kms long, and it is one of the surfers' favourite spots, due to the strength and intensity of its surf. It is also a great place for sunbathers and sand lovers; those who just want to enjoy the beach and the action.

Jacó is not just a beach; it is also a town with all the conveniences and services of modern-day living for visitors, including loads of souvenir shops and restaurants with the most varied international dishes.

Panoramic view of the famous Jacó Beach in the Central Pacific, Puntarenas.

Tourists in the crowded Jacó Beach, known for its intense beach life.

Signs such as this one for surfers, show that Jacó beach is excellent for the practice of this sport.

Bather enjoying the sunset on Jacó beach.

QUEPOS AND MANUEL ANTONIO NATIONAL PARK

Years ago, when the great American Banana Companies had their enormous plantations all around this area, Quepos, 150 Kms from San José, used to be a flourishing port town which monthly received and dispatched great quantities of ships. But when the companies left the area because of a plague that affected the banana plantations, the inhabitants suddenly found themselves without their main source of income. Under the circumstances, other farming activities began to develop, such as the creation of the African palm farms. Fortunately, tourism has now come to be the fastest-growing activity, due mainly to Manuel Antonio National Park, located at a distance of just 7 Kms south of Quepos.

This national park is one of the visitors' favourites, due to the fact that it conjoins beaches with tropical-rainforest environments. Manuel Antonio is one of the smallest National Parks in this country, a place of incomparable scenic beauty; it is a natural island set betwixt great extensions of farmlands. It is common to run into different wild animal species, such as monkeys, toucans, sloths, and "tepezcuintles" (agoutis), along its footpaths.

Quepos is located 150 km of San José.

The beach of Manuel Antonio is located immediately before the entrance to the National Park of the same name.

Manuel Antonio National Park, in the background you can observe the famous 'Catedral' point.

Tourists visiting Manuel Antonio National Park.

The beautiful beaches of Manuel Antonio are among the greatest attractions of this National Park.

DOMINICAL

This is another one of the more popular, beach towns along the Central Pacific, although it is not as popular as Jacó or Quepos. It is located 40 Kms southeast of the latter, right after the mouth of the Barú River. The greatest attractive it offers is its strong surf; surfers are delighted by its intensity, despite the fact that it can be a dangerous beach, due to the suddenness and unpredictability of the currents there. Tourists can also find several natural areas of interest in the vicinity.

Dominical Beach is famous for its strong surf, ideal for this wet sport.

Enthusiastic surfer practising his favourite sport in Dominical Beach.

After surfing, a beautiful sunset, Dominical beach.

Group of seagulls on the beach. Ballena Marine National Park.

Ballena Marine National Park, to the south of the Central Pacific, very important for marine species.

BALLENA ("WHALE") MARINE NATIONAL PARK

This is one of the most recent national parks. Its largest extension, over 5000 hectares, is in the sea, whereas only 110 hectares are terrestrial, in this National Park. It was created with the protection of the Ballena Island Coral Reef and its surroundings in mind, as well as to preserve the reproductive and egg-laying habitat of many species.

Abundant Fauna on the banks of the river Sarapiquí, Northern Plains.

The Northern Plains

The Northern Plains expand North, from the Tilarán and Central mountain ranges, up to the Nicaraguan border, partly occupying territory in two provinces: Heredia and Alajuela. This area has shown important tourist progress in the last years, due mainly to the natural attractions of the great rivers, Sarapiquí, San Carlos and Río Frío, as well as some Natural reserves.

Tourists sailing and photographing species in Caño Negro Lake.

CAÑO NEGRO NATIONAL WILDLIFE REFUGE

Located 36 Kms east of the town of Upala, in the Alajuela canton of the same name, this park, with an extension of just over 10 000 hectares, has acquired a great deal of importance at world level because it is the nesting ground of a huge amount of migratory bird species. It is also the refuge of the "Gaspar", an extraordinary, primitive lunged fish considered a living fossil.

Caño Negro has some bird and plant species that are not found anywhere else in the country. The lake of Caño Negro practically disappears during the dry season, but with the return of the rains, it becomes a sanctuary for a great quantity of birds

An Amazonian kingfisher waits for the opportunity to hunt in Caño Negro.

Emerald green Basilisk in the banks of Caño Negro Lake.

The ardeidos are quite common in the whole area of Caño Negro.

The town of La Fortuna has always had a very active neighbour located right behind it.

LA FORTUNA DE SAN CARLOS

This small town, located on the slopes of Arenal Volcano has lately become one of the country's most important tourist centres, precisely because its greatest attractive is having an active volcano, active since 1968, only 4 Kms away: Arenal Volcano. Beyond having what has come to be considered a beautiful, an almost perfect cone shape, it continuously produces impressive eruptions, in which one can see rocks rolling, gases and lava oozing down the mountainside. Many, highly attractive places are also found in La Fortuna, as well; the tourists relish the thermal water springs and volcanic mud baths due to their well-known benefits to the health. Let us not forget the small and interesting, privately owned natural reserves now established in the area.

Another attraction is Lake Arenal, ideal for the practice of windsurfing, sports fishing, or simply to go for a nice boat ride.

The thermal waters that are found in the base of the Arenal volcano, are really enjoyable to the tourists.

In the area of La Fortuna and lake Arenal, there are many adventure activities that you can go for.

Vista of Arenal Lake and its majestic surrounding vegetation, San Carlos.

Arenal Volcano during an eruption of lava and gases, Arenal Volcano National Park.

Limon fisherman proudly showing off the result of his day's work.

The Caribbean

The Caribbean shoreline area covers an extension that goes from the Nicaraguan border to the north, all the way down to the Panama border in the south. The coastline here is very smooth, compared to that of the Pacific, and it has not been as keenly developed, either, to speak in tourist terms. This whole extension of land is contained inside of the province of Limón. It is a predominantly flat area, mainly to the north of the port city of Limón, but to the south and southeast, there are some hills and mountains, such as Fila De Matama, and part of the Talamanca Mountain Range. Culturally speaking, this whole region differs greatly from the rest of the country. Due, mainly, to the great Jamaican influence of its large black population, distributed all along the Caribbean coastline, with the greatest concentration in the city of Limón.

Colourful heliconia, very typical in the humid tropical area.

Every year, a great quantity of tourists visit Tortuguero National Park in search of its natural attractions.

TORTUGUERO NATIONAL PARK

This is an area of great pluvial precipitations, and there is not a definite dry season, as it happens on the Pacific. Tortuguero is located just between the San Juan River, to the north, and the Parismina River, to the south. It is characterised by its majestic wet tropical rainforest and its labyrinth-like array of canals. The name given to this park derives from the great amount of sea turtles that come to lay their eggs on its beaches. Of the four species that come every year, the Green Turtle is the most common. The boat trip along the canals is quite an adventure, which some connoisseurs have compared with a visit to the Amazon River. From a boat, one can see scores of animal species, reptiles, birds, and mammals. Not mistakenly, this place is actually one of Central America's richest and most bio diverse locations.

Youths of Tortuguero enjoying of a sunny afternoon.

Vista of one of the lagoons of Tortuguero, with its abundant vegetation.

Observant Avetigre with its neck totally extended. Tortuguero National Park.

Many residents of the community of Barra de Tortuguero, make a living from different tourism-related activities.

THE CITY OF LIMÓN

Admiral Christopher Columbus himself arrived, in 1502, on the shore of what today is Limón City. Several centuries later, this city is founded right on the native town of the Cariarí natives

Nowadays, Limón is Costa Rica's most important port. Most of the country's exports and imports pass through this port. For many years, Limón did not have an road that went to the country's centre, and it communicated with the rest of Costa Rica only by train.

This isolation allowed for this province to develop its very own cultural traits, with the influence of the afro-Caribbean diaspora, its music, its food, the people's traditions, and even the spirituality of its inhabitants differs greatly from that of the rest of the country. These characteristics are precisely what make this province a magnet for tourists looking for exotic destinations.

City of Limón with its pier, which can be seen in the background, Costa Rican Caribbean.

Famous Vargas park in the centre of the city in Limón.

SOUVENIRS
SODA
BULEVAR
SOU NIRS
Coca-Cola

Mythic building of the "Black Star Line", one of the oldest buildings of the city of Limón.

Schoolgirls refreshing themselves in a hot day in Limón.

CAHUITA

Located 42 Kms southwest of the city of Limón, Cahuita town is really the Caribbean place to visit; its inhabitants are currently more into tourism activities than into fishing, formerly the town's most important economic activity.

Cahuita's main attraction is the National Park of the same name, famous for its gorgeous coral reef, one of the best on Central America's Caribbean coastline, with more than 140 species of molluscs and 123 species of fish identified, among others. The beautiful white sand beaches, adorned with coconut trees by the thousands are extremely attractive for those who do not care for diving.

Its pristine jungle, categorised as a tropical rainforest, hosts a great number of species of flora and fauna, such as Congo (Howler) Monkeys, raccoons, sloths and many others.

Picturesque town of Cahuita in the south Atlantic, Limón.

The rainbow-billed Toucan is common in Cahuita National Park, just like in other areas of the Atlantic.

In Cahuita National Park, the jungle practically joins the Caribbean Sea.

The crystalline waters of the Caribbean Sea and rustic tourism are among the attractions in Cahuita in the south Atlantic, Limón.

The beaches in Puerto Viejo of Talamanca and its surroundings, are normally of calm and crystalline waters.

PUERTO VIEJO DE TALAMANCA AND COCLES

This famous Caribbean location is only 15 Kms south from Cahuita. Both places conform a group of beautiful beaches 10 Kms long.

Puerto Viejo (Old Harbour) is a small, picturesque hamlet, widely visited, mainly by Europeans and surfers from all over the world.

Another great attraction here is the coral reef area, ideal for the practice of diving and snorkelling, surrounded by spectacular under-water scenery

Lodging options in this area, are mostly rustic and cosy, Puerto Viejo.

Typical architecture of the Caribbean area, with beautiful lively colours, Puerto Viejo.

MANZANILLO

Driving on south, down the same road, and located southeast of Puerto Viejo, is the hamlet of Manzanillo, a small picturesque place, and point of entry into the Manzanillo-Gandoca National Wildlife Refuge. Manzanillo offers its visitors its beautiful, yellow-sand beaches, decorated with rocky promontories here and there, ideal for sunbathing, in addition to a cheerful and hospitable environment. On the other hand, Gandoca-Manzanillo is a refuge, considered of a mixed type, as one can find various habitats, such as, wetlands, reefs, beaches, coconut groves, swamps and others.

This reserve has abundant wildlife, with the great variety of wild waterfowl and birds such as parakeets, parrots, toucans, grasshoppers and many other species.

School children in the small town of Manzanillo, quite near the Gandoca-Manzanillo National Wildlife Refuge. Limón.

Coconut trees, found in great amounts in Gandoca-Manzanillo National Wildlife Refuge.

Fruit and vegetables vendor in Manzanillo.

Punta Mona, famous for its white sand beach and crystalline waters, Gandoca-Manzanillo.

The horse is still one of the most popular means of transport in the rural area. El Brujo.

The South

There are two main roads to get to the South of Costa Rica: the southern Inter American motorway, which passes by Cartago city and along part of the Talamanca Mountain Range, and the Southbound Costanera, going along the Quepos – Dominical coastline route.

This region has the most dramatic topography in the country, from the highest peaks in the Talamanca Mountain Range to the plains of the Valley of Coto Brus, bathed by many rivers, with the Grande de Térraba being the most outstanding.

Another important characteristic is the great quantity of indigenous communities that survived the Colonial period in this area

Typical greengrocer's with traditional products in Palmar Norte.

Palmar Norte is a town on the way to the border with Panamá, south of Costa Rica.

In the forests of the area, precious orchids can still be found.

Hiking, ideal for watching a great variety of birds in San Gerardo de Dota.

THE ZONE OF LOS SANTOS (THE SAINTS)

Southbound, along the Inter American motorway is the zone of Los Santos, (the Saints), thus called, because of the great amount of communities there with several different Saints' names. The most interesting thing about this area is the broken terrain, where great coffee plantations and grazing lands can be seen everywhere.

San Gerardo de Dota is one of the most visited communities due to the trout fishing in the Savegre river, the exuberant natural scenic beauty of this river basin and for being an excellent area for birdwatching, most importantly the beautiful "quetzal".

The basin of the Savegre river is very rich in Cloud Forest vegetation, Llano Azul.

The thick forests in Llano Azul, are frequently swathed in thick fog.

White and crystalline waters of the Savegre River.

SAN GERARDO DE RIVAS AND CHIRRIPÓ NATIONAL PARK

For climbers, and nature lovers, a visit to this park is nothing short of an adventure, the point of departure of which is the town of San Gerardo de Rivas, to set off on the trail-hike that leads to the top of Mount Chirripó.

Town of San Gerardo of Rivas, at the foot of massive Cerro Chirripó.

Typical dwelling and very healthy living habits in San Gerardo de Rivas.

San Gerardo de Rivas is a small mountain hamlet, located some 22 Kms northeast of San Isidro del General. It is a picturesque place at the foot of the Talamanca Mountain Range, in addition to being the departure point for the climb up Mount Chirripó, the visitor can see himself surrounded by the most beautiful scenery, and enjoy the thermal water springs.

The Chirripó National Park has an extension of a little over 50 000 hectares and is located in the middle of The Talamanca Mountain Range. This mountainous park has the highest peaks in the country and they are ideal for the practice of high mountain hiking. Starting the hike in San Gerardo de Rivas, it is possible to reach Chirripó Peak, with a height of 3820 mts (around 12 000 feet) above sea level, the highest in the country.

In the first part of the hike, along a narrow trail, one can see the majestic view of the mountainous scenery of the area, after which, comes up an area covered by a forest of enormous, impressive oaks, all of which is filled with by biodiversity, all along the way. The final part goes along an extensive wasteland, all the way to the top of Mount Chirripó, after 16 arduous Kms of hiking, visitors suddenly find themselves surrounded by lakes and natural terraces carved by ancient glaciers.

'Barba de Viejo' (Old Man's Beard) in the oak trees, on the way to Chirripó National Park.

Tourists on the way to the Cerro Chirripó, walking up one of its main paths.

Enormous oak groves on the way to the Cerro Chirripó.

Panoramic view of the Chirripó National Park, with its lagoons of glacier origin.

Tourist walking back towards San Gerardo de Rivas.

Climbers, after the great effort of arriving at the top of the Chirripó.

Fiesta of the Diablitos, where the inhabitants dress up in allegoric attire, Rey Curré.

INDIAN RESERVES

One of the main characteristics of this area is that it houses a good amount of indigenous communities, descended from the ancient inhabitants of the area, who lived in the territories before and during colonial times. Reserves such as Ujarrás, Salitre, Cabagra, Térraba, Curré, Boruca, and Guaymí are among the most notorious. These small communities have tried all along to safeguard their ancestral legacy through their craftsmanship, their beliefs and traditional celebrations.

Perhaps, the most important celebration for these communities is the "Fiesta de los Diablitos" (the little devils), celebrated in Boruca. The men in the community dress up in colourful attire and carved-wood masks to represent the fight of the aborigines against the Spanish Conquistadors.

Balsa wood mask utilised for the Fiesta of the Diablitos, artisan art Boruca.

Rainforest of Corcovado National Park.

CORCOVADO NATIONAL PARK

This park is located in an area of more than 54 000 hectares in the peninsula of Osa, in the southernmost tip of the country.

This park is considered a living Laboratory, with its wet tropical rainforest, representing one of the last remaining strongholds of this kind of forest in the Mesoamerican Pacific area. Nature scientists who come in search of its huge biodiversity visit the park all year round.

More than 500 tree species can be found there, just inside the park limits, all of them in the most varied of habitats such as: cloud forests, flatland forests and mountain forests, among others. These habitats are the refuge of a great amount of animal species, among which we can mention important populations of felines, red macaws, monkeys, tapirs, crocodiles, toucans, and many others.

Great hiking can be practised in Corcovado National Park.

The rainforest of Corcovado National Park, has great biodiversity.

Visitors in Corcovado National Park, rest after a tiring walk around its forests.

In the forests of this park you can see trees with enormous roots, Corcovado National Park.

Spectacular view of a beach in Corcovado, with its lush rainforest.